Old Glen Prosen and Glen Clova
with neighbouring wee glens and Kirriemuir
John Alexander

Visitors could sample the scenic delights of the glens from coaches operated by Kirriemuir hotels. Here, the Ogilvy Arms coachmen ham it up at the stable doors flanked by posters advertising their tours and fronted by a diminutive wooden horse.

Left: Cortachy Castle interior in 1914, with some fine furnishings on display and a Bath chair in the left foreground.

© John Alexander, 2020
First published in the United Kingdom, 2020,
by Stenlake Publishing Ltd.
www.stenlake.co.uk
ISBN 978-1-84033-882-9

The publishers regret that they cannot supply copies of any pictures featured in this book.

Printed by
P2D, 1 Newlands Road, Westoning, MK45 5LD.

Acknowledgements

Researching Glen Prosen, Glen Clova and the smaller glens has been a delight; one of the joys of compiling a little book like this is that it provides an excuse, if such were needed, to explore these lovely places. In this I was helped by conversations with people on the ground and the splendid efforts made in the run-up to the new millennium by the groups who researched and gathered material relating to the glens and Kirriemuir. They did a wonderful job (see further reading list below). Information has also been culled from Statistical Accounts, Valuation Rolls, church records and other reference material held in Dundee Central Library. Numerous websites were also consulted, notably the National Library of Scotland's map site and Historic Environment Scotland's 'Canmore' site. They are treasures.

Further Reading

The following were the principal books and websites used by the author during his research. Please contact your local bookshop, reference library or search for them on the internet.

Barrie, J. M., *The Little Minister*.
Barrie, J. M., *A Window in Thrums*.
Barrie, J. M., *Auld Licht Idylls*.
Gifford, John, *The Buildings of Scotland: Dundee & Angus*, 2012.
Kirriemuir Millennium Projects Trust, *Kirrie Life*, 2000.
Glens Millennium Group, *Glens Folk*, 2000.
Glens Millennium Group, *Glens Folk Illustrated*, 2000.
Morrison, Dorothy and Reynolds, Isobel, *Rural Schools in Angus*, 2004.
Norrie, James Ltd., *Guide to Thrums*, 1961.

Also by Stenlake Publishing
Mackenzie, Fiona, *Old Kirriemuir*, 2002.

Introduction

Angus is a glorious county. In the east and along the North Sea coast the land is flatter with fields hosting livestock, producing acres of corn or growing berries in abundance, but to the north and west the landscape is different. Initially the change is gradual, but always in the distance is the backdrop of the Grampian Mountains and flowing out of this scenic grandeur are the rivers that over millennia have carved out the lovely Angus Glens. Across the foot of the glens, overlooking the lower ground and backed by the hills, is an irregular strip of verdant country where the great landed families established their estates, built large houses, created ornate parks and, in some cases, held sway for centuries. That some of these families came close to throwing it all away with their support for the Jacobite cause is part of a wider story, as is that of others who rebuilt fortunes in colonial adventures, and built mansions with their new-found wealth.

Meanwhile in the harsher upland environment, farmers battled with the elements and an unforgiving terrain as tenants on land owned by the large estates. This was not crofting country, so small settlements became established at the heads of Glen Prosen and Glen Clova, with slightly larger villages toward the foot. Although the glens were more populous once, they never sustained many people and over time better roads made it as easy for people to leave as to arrive. A question also arises regarding the identity of the early inhabitants because place-names in the glens often reflect Gaelic origins rather than those of the Picts, with which Angus proudly identifies.

In the 19th century the big estates sought to capitalise on the wild landscape and its wildlife by erecting sporting lodges, large hotel-like buildings that came alive in the 'season'. In more modern times people have come, not to shoot or catch the wildlife, but to admire it. Thus the glens have always attracted visitors, be it day-trippers on a picnic, organised youth groups going camping or hostellers utilising the lodges once patronised by the hunters, shooters and fishers. Modern outdoor tourism and event-based activities have since contrived to extend the season throughout the year, with some months simply busier than others.

The 'big town' for the glen communities and great houses alike is Kirriemuir, where a museum celebrating its status as the 'Gateway to the Glens' was opened in 2001. It added to earlier visitor attractions donated by, or dedicated to one of the town's most famous sons, the writer J. M. Barrie, whose best known literary character, Peter Pan, is commemorated by a statue, as is a more recent son, Bon Scott, singer with the rock group AC/DC. Yet such artistic fame can be fickle, and it's hard to imagine the glory of the glens, and Kirrie's place as the 'gateway' being supplanted any time soon.

A young man in Glen Clova holds up a golden eagle that, if the note on the back of the picture is to be believed, he shot by mistake. Good shot, bad mistake!

Kirriemuir was a burgh of barony, a status that allowed it to control all trade within a designated area and hold markets. Its officers could apprehend miscreants and confine them in the tollbooth, or town house, the building where burgh administration was conducted. These activities helped to shape the burgh, with its spacious market square overlooked by the town house, built in 1604 and although altered in shape and stripped of its civic functions in later years, remained as an attractive focus for the square. It is seen here partly obscured by a lorry in a picture from the 1950s. A variety of shops and other businesses used the building for many years, but following a remarkable project set up to mark the millennium it was taken over, given a new lease of life and a new role as the splendid Gateway to the Glens Museum.

There are hints and reminders throughout the town of Kirrie's connections and proximity to the glens. One such was the Ogilvy Arms hotel, a name that pointed to one of the area's most influential families. It sat facing the town house at the corner of High Street as it swung away from the town square toward Glengate, which as the name implies was one of the main routes to and from the glens. The other route, clearly shown in this picture, continued the building line from High Street beside the hotel up the narrow Wee Roods to the Roods where the hotel stables were located. Hotelier Archibald Campbell took over the Ogilvy Arms in 1898 when coach tours were at the height of their popularity, although by the time this undated picture was taken, the coaches had been consigned to history and a new proprietor John Scott had taken over.

Bank Street, seen here in the 1950s, was originally known as St. Mary's Street, but renamed in the 19th century when the British Linen Company set up a bank in the street. The company, which had origins in mid 18th century attempts to encourage the linen industry, did not formally become known as the British Linen Bank until 1906, but by that time the change to the street name had become a fixture, despite some determined local opposition. Part way down the street, in the middle of this picture is another of those reminders of Kirrie's proximity to the glens: the Airlie Garage, which like the Ogilvy Arms reflected the name of one of the area's most prominent families. Established in 1930 the garage moved in 1937 to the site in Bank Street that had been formerly occupied by the Railway Inn.

Bank Street was also the location of a little church that achieved lasting literary fame in J. M. Barrie's books *The Little Minister* and *Auld Licht Idylls*. It was a survivor from the Secession Church founded in 1733 by a group of churchmen who broke away from the Church of Scotland to form a new entity steeped in Covenanting traditions. Imbued with the spirit of dissent, the secessionists subsequently split into a number of other churches while those that remained faithful to the Original Secession became known as the Auld Lichts. Through the 19th century many of these churches reunited, but Kirriemuir's Auld Licht Kirk remained in existence longer than most and had become something of an anachronism when Barrie wrote his stories. The building, which looked as austere as the secessionists' form of worship, was later replaced with one that was used as a Baptist Church, and then shops.

There is one very obvious link to the glens in this late 1950s picture of St. Malcolm's Wynd; facing camera is the Airlie Arms Hotel, the town's oldest inn established in 1760. Like the Ogilvy Arms, it was at one time owned by Archibald Campbell and offered coach trips to the glens for visitors and picnic parties. The picture also shows road signs to the glens, but one connection has disappeared, the street name: St. Malcolm's Wynd was formerly known as Airlie Street. Just beyond the hotel in the centre of the picture, and sporting an Esso sign, is the garage of Barron, King and Lowdon, which was taken over by the Angus Milling Company in the late 1960s and closed some fifteen years later. As with the glens, there are many hints and reminders around the town of the Barrie name; one is seen on the right of this picture.

In the 19th and early 20th centuries the civic focus for the town moved away from the square and town house to Reform Street, seen here looking east from Airlie Street, or St. Malcolm's Wynd, depending on when the picture was taken. A number of public buildings and services were located on the street including a primary school built in 1874, the town hall in 1885 and the library some years later. The street also played host to the police station, courtroom, post office and telephone exchange as well as a wide range of shops. The cobbled street going off to the left, past the prominent corner building in the centre of the picture, is the Roods – a name that is thought to refer to a standard Scots measure for a feu, a plot of ground granted as heritable property on payment of a recurring fee. The Roods went north out of town in the direction of Northmuir and beyond there to the glens.

Development of Kirriemuir's other muirs (moors), Forestmuir, Southmuir, Westmuir and Northmuir, began in the early 19th century. Northmuir is seen here about 1910 with the house known as Anglepark in the centre of the picture. The building style suggests that it predated the other cottages in the picture, but the name lives on in modern street names. Development generally appears to have been sparse at the time the picture was taken, but behind the wall in the left foreground are what look like the fences of animal pens for the livestock markets located here. Later described in a guidebook as having 'scattered cottages each with a garden gay with flowers', Northmuir has since been widely developed for housing and has also become the location of a primary school, built in 1977 to replace the old school in Reform Street.

Glengate takes a route in and out of Kirriemuir that broadly follows the course of the Gairie Burn, which flowed from the Loch of Kinnordy and helped to shape the town and its industries. One of those industries, the Meikle Mill is seen in this picture taken about 1909, the time it was acquired by J. A. Whamond and Sons. The company also converted the former Kirk o' Relief in Glengate to mill oatmeal. Renamed the Angus Milling Company in 1938, they also began marketing the Meikle Mill's rolled oats as 'Peter Pan Oats', based on the name of J. M. Barrie's most famous character. He was the boy who never grew up, which perhaps made it a slightly contradictory name for a food regarded as helpful for growing children. Following the company's take-over by the large Hamlyn Milling Company in 1976 the Peter Pan name was dropped and, some fifteen years later, oat milling in Kirrie came to an end.

J. M. Barrie set some important scenes in his book *The Little Minister* in Caddam Wood, which lies in close proximity to Northmuir and also, on its western edge to Causewayend where this splendid 'smithy' was situated. There are a number of places in Scotland named Causewayend, or Causewayhead – in effect where causewayed, or cobbled, streets ended and dirt roads began. The smithy was probably well sited at such a location and the building with its inverted horseshoe architrave around the door looks splendid, as does the handsome heavy horse. The picture dates from about 1905 when the blacksmith was James McGregor – he could be the man in the picture. The smithy's location at Causewayend was on the Kinnordy Estate close to where the drive to and from the big house joined the road.

Kinnordy House, the large mansion in this picture from about 1900, is situated just to the north west of Kiriemuir. It was rebuilt about 1880/1881 on almost exactly the same site as an earlier house that had belonged to the Ogilvy family who moved there from Inverquarity Castle. They sold the property in 1782 to Charles Lyell, who had made his fortune as a naval contractor. Subsequent generations of the Lyell family distinguished themselves in scientific pursuits; Charles Lyell II was a notable botanist and his son, also Charles, a geologist. Members of the family also played prominent roles in Kirriemuir life. Tragedy struck in 1943 when the then head of the family, Charles Antony Lyell was killed as he led an attack on an artillery and machine gun post while fighting with the Scots Guards in North Africa. He was awarded a posthumous Victoria Cross for his bravery. Seventy years later the Lyells sold Kinnordy to new owners.

To the north of Kinnordy is the village of Carroch seen here in a picture from about 1907. The bridge in the foreground spans the Quarity Burn from which water was drawn off to provide power to a couple of mills adjacent to the village. A little school was built at Carroch in 1875 in response to the Education Act of 1872, which required all children between the ages of five and thirteen to go to school, although at about the time this picture was taken inspectors were berating the local school authorities for the poor standard of its desks and seats. With sparsely populated catchment areas, rural schools were always going to struggle for resources. The school was a little to the north of the village and even further north was a small reservoir for the Kirriemuir Water Works.

About a mile north of Carroch is Pearsie, an estate with mansion, steadings and other outbuildings on the west bank of Prosen Water. A smaller, older house stood on the property before 1805 when it was remodelled to form the imposing three-storey building, with its piended-roof and bow-frontage seen in this photograph taken almost exactly 100 years after the rebuilding. The estate was the property of the Wedderburn family, some of who harboured Jacobite sympathies while others later gave the family fortunes a boost by supporting British rule in India. Charles Wedderburn (1748-1829), who inherited the property and had served in India, commissioned the rebuilding work. In more modern times the estate has diversified, with the outbuildings being utilised for leisure lettings.

The Earl of Angus granted Lednathie to Alexander Ogilvy of Inverquarity in 1434 but when he was killed the property reverted to the earl before being again granted to the Ogilvy family. The estate was leased in 1648 to a James Farquharson who held it for 35 years. The next lessee, James Stormonth converted it to freehold in 1712 and the family, later known as Stormonth-Darling, has retained the property ever since eventually establishing their residence at one of the houses, Easter Lednathie. The old building there was demolished in 1831, rebuilt and then extended a few years later. This picture, taken *circa* 1910, shows the house adorned with a tower and battlements. These features were added in 1878, but by the 1930s the battlements were found to be too heavy for the walls and taken down. The tower remained in place until 1958.

At Lednathie the road splits, with a minor branch heading west to Wester Lednathie and into Glen Uig. It continues as a hill track before crossing the watershed and descending south by way of Glen Quarity. The main line of the Glenprosen road heads north from Lednathie up and over the shoulder of Broom Hill descending to Wester Dalinch and Spott Bridge, which links the roads on the west and east sides of the glen. It is seen here in a picture from the late 1920s. Just across the bridge, but out of picture to the right, the imposing Spott House and the farm occupy a rare patch of level ground on the east side of the glen. To the north of Spott Bridge the road stays on the west bank of the Prosen Water for about three miles eventually crossing the river near the head of the glen, just before Glenprosen Lodge.

The number of sporting estates in Scotland's hill country grew through the Victorian era. Indeed, by acquiring Balmoral and popularising a romantic image of the Highlands the Queen contributed to this process as wild and remote corners of the country were turned over to hunting, shooting and fishing. To service this activity a new kind of building, the shooting lodge, began to appear in locations that were often well away from 'the beaten track'. The advent of railways greatly aided the growth of sporting estates by providing a means for the, usually wealthy, tenants and their guests to get to within a carriage ride of the estate. Slotting neatly into this timescale and way of life was Glenprosen Lodge. Built in the mid 19th century, and perhaps better known locally as Craig Lodge, it was typical of such additions to the upland landscape.

With no prominent landmark, there is little to identify this picture other than a hand-written note on the back: 'Glen Prosen, Angus, Aug. 1929'. It could have been penned by one of the two men in the picture, but who were they? Clad in well-worn tweeds, they look comfortable on the hills. The one with a bag over his shoulder and leaning on a shooting stick could be a keeper, while the other has dogs at his heel. They look like Labradors, regarded at the time as perhaps the best all-round dog on game shoots. Other retrievers, like spaniels, were also popular, but when deep heather covered the moors, pointers and setters were often preferred. The men and dogs look at home in this environment, but the boy perched on a shooting stick and clothed in a suit and cap of matching tweed has the resigned look of someone who would rather be somewhere else.

A couple of miles south of Craig Lodge on the eastern side of the glen is this imposing house, Balnaboth. It is a name derived from Gaelic: 'bal, or bally' – a settlement, 'na' – of the, 'both or bothy' – a hut, so a hutted settlement perhaps? Such a name could have ancient origins or simply refer to the house, which also conforms to that description. It was created about 1824 when Donald Ogilvy of Clova set about amalgamating four existing structures of varying dates, the earliest from the 16th century. The dominant element of this combined structure was the west wing, which is seen with its gable facing the camera in the centre of this picture. The large porch was probably added later in the 19th century.

The road to Balnaboth house is seen on the left of this view of Glenprosen village with on the right, Inchmill, a centre of estate activity including a blacksmith's forge. The building also formerly housed the Glenprosen Post Office and was fulfilling that function in 1924 when someone wrote on the back of this picture postcard: 'We stopped at this Post Office and got some lemonade' – sadly the message did not record whether the sender had also bought and posted the card at the post office. Telephone calls were also routed through the post office until that function was superseded in the 1960s by a local exchange, and not long after that the post office itself was closed.

Entering Glenprosen village from the south, the road crosses the little bridge over the burn. The building in the background is Glentarie Shooting Lodge. It was small compared to the Craig Lodge, but shared some characteristics. The advantages of electricity came late. Balnaboth House and Glentarie were both wired in the 1920s and initially powered with a diesel generator and batteries, before mains power arrived in 1961 courtesy of the North of Scotland Hydro-Electric Board. Much of the village was also fed off the Glentarie system, but prior to any of that, the occupants of lodges, houses and other buildings had to rely on oil lamps and candles. Life in the glens was not easy.

Glentarie Lodge is in the centre of this view of Glenprosen village. The manse is on the right, with the church, a simple whitewashed box-like structure dating from 1802 on slightly lower ground between it and the main village. This was not the minister's only church, he had another at Clova, and serving both involved trekking through the gap in the hills behind the village. The route, covering six miles of rough and, in places, steep terrain became known as the 'minister's path'. This kind of ministry was funded through the Royal Bounty, a fund set up in 1725 and provided annually by the Crown to employ itinerant missionary ministers in remote parts of the country to spread Protestant teachings and guard against Catholicism. In more modern times the 'minister's path' has become popular with walkers visiting the glens.

The 'minister's path' joined the track on the west side of Glen Clova near Newbiggin, to the south of Caddam where this flock of sheep was photographed. With shepherds, dogs and children, and some animals happily munching the lush verges, it looks quite relaxed, but farming in the glens was not for the faint hearted. Some farms had fields on flatter ground near the rivers that could be put into crops, but the hilly marginal ground was stocked with cattle or sheep, mainly sheep. Horses were the principal motive power and farms were often measured by how many animals it took to work the land, rather than the number of acres. That began to change after the Second World War with the introduction of tractors, and in more modern times the quad bike; one of them could have quickly driven this flock to wherever it was going.

Ministers, shepherds and other road users had to cross the river to get to Clova village. They could use a ford when conditions allowed or cross dry-shod, just upstream, on this rickety-looking suspension footbridge. Such hazards were consigned to history at the latter end of the 19th century when a stone bridge was erected. The need for ministers to trek back and forth between the glens also ended by the middle of the 19th century when Clova was made a 'quoad sacra' parish – one with religious, but not civil responsibilities. A new Clova church was erected in 1855 and a new manse, seen here beyond the footbridge was also built. The parishes were again united under one minister in 1946 making the manse redundant. It was sold as a private house and has since been adapted as a holiday let.

From Clova, a minor road heads into the hills for about three miles to a point where the glen splits either side of steep mountains, with the branch to the north west, round the base of Craig Mellon, known as Glen Doll. A small group of buildings occupied the area at the confluence of the burns, one of which was the imposing Glendoll Lodge. Formerly, as the name implies, a shooting lodge, it was taken over as an 80-bed youth hostel after the Second World War, replacing an earlier facility, a wooden chalet at Newbiggin. Situated in the heart of the hills at 1,000 feet above sea level the lodge was well placed to cater for those outdoor activities the Scottish Youth Hostels Association liked to encourage: walking, climbing, skiing and field studies. And if the hostellers weren't exhausted after their exertions, the building also had a squash court.

Clova was known as both a mill town and a kirk town although in reality it was never more than a village with a kirk and a mill. It also had that other essential of village life, a post office, which was situated, beside a track leading off the Glen Doll road and is seen here with the distinctive bulk of Ben Reid behind. Arntibber, an old name for the locality, was also given to the house. In the early years of the 20th century the postmistress was Mrs Duncan, but when she died Mrs Cameron took over, a role she carried on for many years, later moving, with the post office business, to the old manse. The postal service was clearly in the family blood because her daughter Jean became the glen postie and 'made a name for herself' by (shock, horror!) wearing trousers, or slacks as such female garments were known at the time.

Clova attracted a wide range of people intent on exploring the hills and enjoying the wild landscape. Some, like Guides, Scouts and the Boys Brigade, came in organised groups to set up camp, while others were drawn to the more comfortable accommodation at the Ogilvy Arms Hotel (not to be confused with the hotel of the same name in Kirriemuir). Established in the mid 19th century, the hotel was a prominent feature of the village. Guests could enjoy the full range of country sports, or less strenuously take a carriage ride to local scenic routes and attractions. Later renamed as the Clova Hotel, it has, in modern times, been adapted to the changing tastes of visitors with a range of self-catering lodges equipped with sauna, hot tub and dish washers – a different world to sleeping under canvas and scrubbing dishes in the cold water of a burn or river.

The river that rolls down Glen Clova is the South Esk, one of many 'Esks' in Scotland, a name that simply means water. Nearly 50 miles long, it is the largest river in Angus with headstreams that tumble down from the southern Grampians to form a substantial river by the time it is joined by the White Water, just below the Glen Doll lodge, at Braedownie. Numerous burns emanating from every hillside corrie and deeper glen add to the flow and it is further swollen by its largest tributary, the Prosen Water, as it heads on through Strathmore to the sea at Montrose. It has many faces, in places turbulent, in others tranquil and meandering. Here it wins its way past some rocks near Clova village where a group of well-dressed children pose for the camera and an adult keeps watch in the background from the old suspension footbridge (shown on page 25).

On the east side of the glen south of Clova is Inchdowrie House, which was built in 1914 in the Arts and Crafts style and is noted for its sunken garden. Further south is Wheen Farm, but the largest, most imposing structure is Rottal Lodge, seen here in a picture from the 1920s, or 1930s and described in a guidebook of 1902 as 'the white shooting-lodge of Rottal'. Formerly Lord Airlie's property, the estate was sold about 2008 and although still used for its earlier purpose of shooting, fishing and farming, the buildings have been adapted to cater for a range of functions including as a venue for weddings, corporate events and holiday lets. The owners have even installed a 450kW hydroelectric scheme.

A hand-written note on the back of this charming picture identifies the subjects as the 'Misses Robbie of Gella Farm', which has a high probability of being correct, as successive generations of the Robbie family were tenant farmers at Gella. It was/is a sizeable farm, part of the Earl of Airlie's estates about two and a half miles south of Rottal, and this picture of two young women each holding a lamb could be a big clue as to what the farm's main, or at least one of its main activities was at the time, but what time? The only dating evidence is the sisters' clothing, which could be as late as the 1920s, perhaps Edwardian – it's a tricky call, the glens were unlikely to have been at the forefront of fashion.

The pictures on this page and the facing page were found mounted on the pages of a Victorian atlas along with the one of the Misses Robbie overleaf. The only other clue to their identity is the word 'Clova' that whoever did this wrote beside them, so it is not certain if they were taken at Gella Farm, or another location in the glen. The people in the picture are all dressed for the occasion, but not the part they are playing. Although the woman is holding a rake, she doesn't appear to have created the little haystack and the fishing rods being held by the boys and young man would have been of little use in a field. Perhaps that's why the boys look bored, keen to try their luck down on the river, which was described in an early guidebook as looking 'very fishful'. The South Esk was, indeed still is, a noted salmon river.

These photographs look to have been taken with a large plate camera. They are well composed, in this one a plant hides dead space in the foreground and none of the people masks anyone else, only the woman with the teapot is looking warily at the camera, as if she has chosen the wrong moment to check her position. The boy pouring milk from the jug and the woman holding the cup and saucer have got it just right, and yet the picture doesn't look posed. The photographer clearly knew what he or she was doing, perhaps a professional. That and the style and quality of the clothes, suggests that these were people of means, possibly visitors or holidaymakers who wanted to take away a memorable moment from their time in the glen.

With a title of 'The Parting of the Ways, Glen Clova' this picture is taken looking north from the junction where the glen roads meet, or diverge depending on the direction of travel. The road to the left sticks to the west side of the glen, the right hand road to the east and they meet again at Clova. In 1932, when this picture was taken, there will almost certainly have been less traffic than in later years and the photographer has either got lucky with a passing car or persuaded a driver, maybe his own driver, to stop at the best spot. To the right of the car, half-hidden by trees is the Gella Bridge, a single arched masonry structure spanning the South Esk that has since been replaced by a modern bridge complemented by picnic places on both banks.

To the north of Gella Bridge, on the west side of the glen, is the likely location of this picture entitled 'Wateresk Picnic 1908'. Communal picnics were popular forms of entertainment in Victorian and Edwardian days and the glens were always favourite spots. People belonging to church groups or other associations would gather in Kirriemuir and be whisked out to the glens in horse-drawn vehicles, and later in charabancs, for a fun day out. Although the picture is of poor quality and slightly blurred, it is a delightful image. A mat of some kind appears to have been laid out on the grass so that the people could dance to the music of a piper. Wateresk was also the location of a little school and schoolhouse, which sat in close proximity to Braeminzion Farm and had ready access to a footbridge over the river.

There is another parting of the ways at Dykehead where the roads for Glen Clova and Glen Prosen diverge. On the latter, just outside the village is Burnside Lodge. One resident who became well-known was Dr Edward Wilson, a junior doctor and zoologist on the 1901-04 British National Antarctic Expedition, otherwise known as the *Discovery* expedition, led by Captain Robert Falcon Scott. He was later engaged by the government to conduct a survey into diseases in the grouse population and, while working on that, stayed at Burnside Lodge. Scott visited Wilson while he was there and together the two men planned the expedition to the South Pole on board the *Terra Nova* in 1911-12 that proved fatal for both. A splendid carved cairn has been erected beside the Glen Prosen road as a memorial to them.

The memorial cairn erected to honour Wilson and Scott replaced an earlier granite fountain that had been damaged after a few encounters with motor vehicles and vandals. A plaque from the original fountain was incorporated in the modern cairn. Another, more conspicuous, memorial sits atop Tulloch Hill just behind Burnside Lodge. Designed to echo the shape of the tower of the ruined Airlie Castle in Glen Isla, it commemorates the 11th Earl of Airlie who was killed in 1900 leading his cavalry regiment in a charge at the Battle of Diamond Hill during the South African, or Boer, War. The war did not go well for the regular army and home defence regiments including the local mounted infantry unit, the Fife and Forfar Yeomanry were called into action. It was the first time that part-time civilian soldiers had served overseas; the next time was in 1914-18, which resulted in another memorial erected to honour the men of Cortachy and Clova.

Built in 1887, the Royal Jubilee Hotel, or as it was later known, the Dykehead Hotel, was a focal point for people from the glens, although in the early days holidaymakers will have provided some custom, stopping off while observing the scenery from the comfort (if that's the right word) of a horse-drawn carriage. Comfort was perhaps not the hotel's strongest selling point, described in an early guidebook as 'a road-side house with a beer and porter license, a sitting room and a hammock'. Later, and as a much-extended building, it enjoyed a halcyon period when, with live entertainers, dinner-dances and ceilidhs, it became a social centre for people from well beyond the area. It couldn't last, and in common with rural pubs and hotels all over the country the building, its music and all the life that went with it have gone.

Situated at Dykehead on the opposite side of the road to the hotel, and a bit further south, Cortachy Post and Telegraph Office also doubled as a village shop. Such an arrangement was not unusual in rural locations, but the type of shop that operated alongside this post office was somewhat different because in 1904, when the picture was taken, James Winter the proprietor and postmaster was also a draper and when people bought their stamps and postal orders they could also buy clothes. Cortachy Post Office also acted as the postal distribution point for the glens. Bags of mail, made up in Kirriemuir, were sent to Cortachy where the glen's posties collected them for onward delivery to local addresses and to the post offices at Glenprosen and Clova.

With the South Esk to the north and Prosen Water to the south, Cortachy Castle sits on the narrowing neck of land between the rivers as they flow to their confluence just beyond the building. It looks like a good defensive location although the castle is more stately home than fortification. James, 7th Lord Ogilvie and future 1st Earl of Airlie, acquired the castle from a kinsman in 1625, and then made it his principal residence in 1642 after Airlie Castle in Glen Isla was burned. That was done as a reprisal for his Royalist stance during the Covenanting wars and successive Earls continued to support the Stuart cause through the Jacobite rebellions of 1715 and 1745. Somehow they managed to retain Cortachy as the family home, which, much modified over the years, is seen here in a picture from about 1910. The little tower on the extreme right is the oldest part of the house.

Cortachy House was built as a manse in the 1860s, as part of a wider change to estate management credited to Blanche, Countess of Airlie. She wanted the estate factor to be close to the castle rather than being based at Lintrathen, at the foot of Glen Isla, where much of the family's estates were situated. The new manse allowed the minister to move out of the older, late 18th century, manse so that it could be used by the factor. In the mid 20th century, as the churches contracted, the Cortachy minister had a heavy Sunday workload, starting in the local church in the morning, preaching at Memus in the middle of the day and alternating between Glen Prosen and Glen Clova churches in the afternoon. With further church amalgamations the manse at Cortachy became surplus to requirements and has since become a bed and breakfast establishment.

The little Cortachy Church is seen here in a picture from 1930 with the ornate north gate of Cortachy Castle beyond it, to the left. Built to the designs of architect David Paterson, the church was erected by the 9th Earl of Airlie in 1828/29 on a site formerly occupied by a medieval church. The Airlie family has a memorial aisle at the church. In 1999, as congregations dwindled, the little church at Cortachy became part of the united parish of The Glens and Kirriemuir Old, thus keeping the building functioning as a place of worship. Just beyond the castle gate the road crosses the South Esk and just downstream from the bridge, is a large boulder, the 'Deil's Stane'. Legend has it that the minister of Cortachy went up the glen where he encountered the devil. An argument ensued and the devil threw the boulder at the church, but the minister managed to deflect it with his crucifix so that it missed the target and landed in the river. It must have made quite a splash!

Situated on the north bank of the South Esk and overlooking its confluence with the Prosen Water is Downie Park, a harled and slated mansion house with a bowed frontage visible in this picture from the 1930s or 40s. The house probably dates from very early in the 19th century, not long after William Rattray, a retired Indian Army officer, bought the small estate. Originally from Perthshire he had gone to India, along with his brother James, keen to revive the family fortunes lost through adherence to the Jacobite cause. Returning to Scotland, he had ambitions to establish a new Rattray dynasty, but it didn't work out as he hoped. He died in 1819 and was buried on the estate close to the river: too close, because a flood disturbed the grave. His tomb was later erected at The Howff, in Dundee. The Earl of Airlie acquired Downie Park in 1871.

Inverquarity Castle occupies the narrow point of land between the River South Esk and Quarity Burn as they flow toward their confluence a few hundred yards to the east. Erected early in the 15th century for a branch of the Ogilvy family, the castle was further strengthened mid century when King James II granted Alexander Ogilvy licence to fortify it and erect an iron yett (gate). It remained the family's main residence until the late 17th century when they moved to Kinnordy, effectively abandoning the old fortress. Part of the structure that formed an L shape with the main tower was demolished in subsequent years to provide stone for the adjacent farm steading – the broken wall ends easily visible in this picture from about 1910. Restoration in the early 1970s brought the castle back from potential ruin.

Downstream from where the waters of the South Esk and Quarity Burn join together, another tributary, the White Burn adds to the flow. Just below that confluence the river is spanned by Shielhill Bridge, the splendid single-arched structure seen in this picture, which dates from 1904 or earlier. The bridge was erected about 1769/70 to carry the road that runs between Kirriemuir and all points east to Noranside. It was in use for just over 200 years before being superseded by a modern concrete arched structure, built by contractor William Briggs. The Earl of Airlie formally opened the new bridge on 10th August 1973, leaving the old one standing as a glorious monument to the skills of 18th century craftsmen.

About a mile to the north of Shielhill Bridge and a couple of miles east of Downie Park is the little village of Memus. It is seen here looking north around the 1920s with Burnside in the background, where the village school was located. Judging by the number of bicycles in the picture, these appear to have been the preferred means of transport for the men who have gathered around the post office, the building on the left. The church is on the right. It was built as the Free Church of Tannadice following the Disruption of 1843, a major schism that split the Church of Scotland and led to the formation of the Free Church. The little Memus church became a United Free Church in 1900 and, following church reunion in 1929, returned to the Church of Scotland. In 1945 the Memus and Cortachy churches were united, with the minister also assuming responsibility for part of Tannadice Parish that included Glen Moy and Glen Quiech.

There are a number of glens called Glen Quiech, thought to be so-named because their geographic shape resembles a quaich (drinking cup) – plausible, but is it true? Some names of farms and houses in Glen Quiech, in Angus, are certainly distinctive: Rashiebog, Horniehaugh, Anniegathel and Scalywell. More prosaic was the big house named 'Glen Quiech' at the foot of the glen, seen in this picture from the 1930s. It was, for a time, the home of the MacLagan family whose soldier son, Ewan George Sinclair MacLagan served in India and fought in the South African War before being posted to Australia, back to the UK, then 'Down Under' again where he taught at the Royal Military College of Australia, Duntroon, the country's Sandhurst. He commanded Australian troops at Gallipoli and on the Western Front during the First World War, before retiring as a much-decorated Major General. He had the honour of unveiling the Tannadice Parish War Memorial in August 1920.

To the east and slightly south of Glen Quiech House is the narrow Den of Ogil Reservoir, which was formed to provide a water supply for the Burgh of Forfar and parts of Forfar and Glamis Parishes. The plans, prepared by John F. Bateman, one of the leading water industry engineers at the time, were presented for approval to Parliament in 1877. They sought powers to take water from the White Burn as well as utilising the stream flowing through the Den of Ogil. The proposal was to create two dams, or embankments, just over 100 yards in length, one to the east and another in the west, to contain both ends of the reservoir. The plans also provided for aqueducts to convey the water to Forfar and road access, as seen here in a picture showing the east end of the reservoir. With subsequent changes to the structure of the water supply industry the reservoir has since come under the management of Scottish Water. It is a well-regarded trout fishing venue.